MORE GOD THAN DEAD

Lori,

I t has been a pleasure getting to Know you over these past several months. You are a blessing to Rock Hill. I look forward to Seeing even more great things. Thanks for the support!

ANGELO GETER

MORE GOD THAN DEAD

ANGELO GETER

EDITED BY

ED MADDEN

The Laureate Series

Library of Congress Number: 2022938727
ISBN: **978-1-942081-30-2**

Cover Art by Keela Lewis

More God Than Dead is the Fourth book in the Laureate
Series, an endeavor by Muddy Ford Press to celebrate the
tradition of poetry that is born to South Carolinians, and to
promote and honor the relationship between
Mentor and Protégé,
Advocate and Postulant,
Poet and Poet.

The Laureate Series

Table of Contents

This collection is dedicated to my late wife Jasmine Teshay Jackson Geter. (1989-2017). Affectionately known as Jas, J, Mash, Jasze, and Aunt J. I am thankful for the years we shared on this earth.

This collection is also dedicated to those who have lost a spouse. Loss does not and will not define you.

I

Ritual

When a brown body is swallowed by the ground
it once claimed as home, the clocks stop ticking.

Eulogies are written between sobs, tongues held
for a ransom no one has the emotional currency to pay.

Voices are kidnapped by the thief of silence,
the house turns into a family reunion of bodies gathering

to reclaim the blood that has been lost
before more is spilled from the same roots.

When a brown body becomes prey,
the living room is a buffet of casseroles and wrinkled

silver pans crowded with chicken still golden
and percolating from the sauna of heat.

The skin speaks in a sharp sizzle, the scent
conquers the room where the dead person's

family, whose bodies—now empty from grief
are looking for something to be filled with.

On the back porch, Hennessy is passed around like an heirloom,
poured into cups the same color as blood, while

some relative everyone knows tells
a story no one has ever heard,

and an earthquake of laughter erupts
loud enough to drown the sobbing.

The cups dip and drip liquor the same hue as their skin,
quenching spirits who can no longer drink for themselves.

A man pulls a black & mild out of his pocket,
 and uses a blade to remove the guts.

He fills it with the same earth his feet are resting on,
folding until the ends finally meet. On the front porch,

bouquets of lilies flood the entrance in a sea of white.
Brown hands lift them inside and swell the room

until there is no space left to stand
or breathe.

Ghazal on Grief

The world spins endlessly when you are reeling on the axis of grief.
You lose your balance and pain has you spilling your grief.

Tears swirl into a monsoon of wreckage.
Tidal waves quickly ravage all your feelings of grief.

Loved ones will extend their olive branch arms,
yet anxiety will have you concealing the grief.

They will tell you that God doesn't make mistakes,
but faith is hard to keep when you are kneeling in grief.

You will stumble and trip religiously, falling
over parables of depression as you start unveiling this grief.

After the brick and mortar of your life is dismantled,
normalcy will start congealing from the debris of grief.

You will question the future,
but you will survive Angelo. There is healing after grief.

5 stages
after Donte Collins

Denial
>   My wife is not dead
>   Dead   not
>   my wife is
>   Is   my
>   Wife   dead

Anger
>   I hate you forever God
>   God   you
>   Forever   hate
>   forever
>   I   hate   God

Bargaining
>   Bring her back here now
>   bring her back
>   Now her
>   Bring   her
>   Here now

Depression
>   I am nothing without her
>   I   am   nothing
>   Without her
>   Am I
>   nothing

Acceptance

      My wife is
God   forever
  bring her back
          Here now
  I am

Denial

is the lump simmering beneath plump skin,
is distraction instead of diagnosis,
is a CD skipping to a rhythm
it was not intended to play,
is the black bonnet I never washed,
is the toothbrush laying
in the last place she stood whole.

North Star

My wife lays
on a hospital bed.
Her body unraveled,
scabbed and scathed
from cold scalpels searing
through warm dark flesh.
Her incisions are bloody
constellations against
a black night.
A roadmap to freedom yet
she is a slave here.
Shackled to a disease
that treats her intestines
like a burning cross.
A lynching without
the luxury of knowing
who holds the noose.
I watch her lie still
and desperately long
to be her North Star,
Underground Railroad,
compass or key
to escape the body
attempting to evict her.
I am no landlord of bones.
Just an abolitionist
looking to emancipate
her from this oppression
before this vessel
buries her alive.

Sonnelegy: Unfiltered

When they buried her with casket dipping
like hydraulics descending in darkness,
I felt all my fuel being siphoned.
The octane in this unleaded heart was
funneled through a dark filter of despair.
No engines can function on fumes alone.
A vehicle has no purpose without
something to fill it with— a way to move.
She was the momentum that pushed this love.
Her eyes were steering wheels that guided
compass hands leading to new direction.
A melanated road map of tough skin
and sacrifice. A shea butter angel
with coiled halo, driving towards heaven.

A Few Things Jasmine Taught Me

stone-washed jeans don't go
with light colored shirts.
how to part hair like a red
sea with grease and a plastic comb.
emergency room chairs hold
fear better than flesh.
an extra large apple juice
slush from Sonic(s) is the
holiest thing your tongue
will drown in. leftovers
are the devil's appetizers.
a country girl's tongue
is sharper than any blade
that will kiss your face.
walking in high heels
is a delicate artform few
practice correctly. long
hair really doesn't care.
Patrón margaritas will
make for good laughs
and terrible hangovers.
hospital is really pronounced
hahs-spee-tull. icu waiting
rooms smell like anxiety.
Crohn's disease burns
your intestines like a furnace.
melanin can conjure spells
without chanting a word.
north Carolina AT&T

does indeed have the greatest
homecoming on earth. black
women wear resilience
like a fashion statement.
pettiness and shade
are a language
all their own.
black love is a privilege
always worth fighting for.

Vows I

To the love of my life
Here we are again in a place as beautiful as this
In a time as special as this
In a world as crazy as this is
Today we are joining our hands and hearts together as one
Binding this tangible love into a supernatural experience

Today is an amazing day
But not for the reasons most people think
Not because of the flowers or the drapery
Not because of the songs, the color scheme or cutlery
Not because of the way your makeup is contoured to your face
Not because of the way your dress accentuates your hips
Not because we are being watched and observed
Not for the food, music or dancing

But today is beautiful simply because we are alive
Simply Because we have made it
Because the blood is running warm in our veins
It is beautiful because there is a sparkle of God in your eyes
That makes me bow down and pray to your majesty
Today I worship the queen in you
The Nefertiti in your walk
The CleoPatra in your tongue
The Sheba in your stride

I sink into   skin and

  exodus

    the

                              heart
This is
A new beginning

God

  will

Makes essays out of words

I will hand write our love story
And promise not to **plagiarize** **our** happiness
This **marriage** will not be graded on a curve
Which means that I will earn you
I will work for every smile
Every laugh
Every hug
Every kiss

I will work for you
And you will work for me
So that we can work for him
And when the day comes
I will be your Valedictorian
Summa Cum laude student
Dedicated to graduating to the next step our love together
Forever

Depression

is the kid at school
who everyone knows
but no one acknowledges.
We ignore him
because we are afraid
of what will happen
when he finally says hello.

Alternate Names for Death
after Danez Smith

1. thief of laughter and light
2. one who stalks life in the shadows
3. necessary
4. enemy of memories
5. me
6. black bodies coated in smoke
7. bruised carcass of heart
8. (insert name here)
9. refuge of the fallen
10. me...again
11. conjoined twin of birth
12. echo of joy
13. addiction
14. an unlikely home
15. the leopard pillowcase drenched in my wife's scent

Black Grief is a Seance

Black grief is the inside joke America puts on mute.
A silent film no one has the attention span to watch
unless the body is soaked in gunpowder thrown from foreign hands.

Timelines and status updates flash the dead names
like a marquee, while the hashtag is hungry to add more to its collection.
If the grief isn't sexy or comical we don't have space for it here.

If the chest wasn't seared by a bullet,
or neck mangled from a noose
it isn't worth the airtime.

If the man's heart stopped thumping,
if the woman's blood clotted to infinity,
if the boy's cells sickled a symphony of submission,

if the girl's lungs howled into the wind,
the channel gets turned before the broadcast even begins.

Black grief is a rite of passage.
We are taught the weight of death
before our legs sprint towards playgrounds and jungle gyms.

We know that someday soon someone who looks like us
will become corpse before their 16th birthday.
We know that it could very easily be us.

Whether through cancer or traffic stop,
our lives can fade into a darkness heavier
than the melanin our skin holds.

So we treat death like a celebration.
Call it a Home-going instead of a funeral.
Dance until the ancestors shake beneath us.

Cry until the sobs become songs.
Pray as though the body sitting at the front
of the church can actually hear us.

Black grief is thicker than grandma's cornbread,
tangier than Carolina barbecue,
saltier than collard greens simmering over swollen heat.

It is a gospel song coated in regret,
a Mahalia Jackson wail,
Marvin Sapp singing *Never Would've Made It*
without knowing if we actually will.

Shots

1.
Liquor is the world's
oldest form of medicine.
We get drunk to heal

2.
Jack Daniels and Coke
are the only deities
worth dying here for.

3.
My bartender Mike
is a benevolent god
who resurrects me.

4.
If I am a drunk
then grief must be the chaser
that keeps me alive.

5.
I'm drinking so much
I forget that sober feels
like being human.

Top Shelf

Alcohol is the god who rides shotgun
when everyone else has decided to walk home.
It never abandons.

When my lips sink into its mouth,
when the night air becomes colder than vacant bedsheet,
it lights a bonfire in my throat.

Jesus is at the bottom of every bottle,
so I keep drinking to reach salvation.
A slave choosing the whip instead of a way.

When the pain is Absolut,
the Crown doesn't seem as Royal.
The Skyy doesn't look like heaven.

Jager bombs my face until the body becomes Hypnotic.
Painkillers twist Screwdrivers in my chest,
while Hurricanes turn White Russians into Zombies.

I always forget that the proof is in the proof.
That memories haunt like ghosts
conjuring up top shelf skeletons.

They call them spirits because they Lazarus my demons.
Turn a binge into a séance.
Body shots into a crime scene.

There are days when I'd rather believe
in José Cuervo than JesuCristo.
Patrón is stronger than Proverbs.

Psalms ain't enough
but Paul Masson is.
This is when I meet my Maker's Mark,

Isolate in distilleries of doubt,
vomit scriptures in a bathroom stall
and kneel before a porcelain altar that feels like home.

If I Die Here Tonight

Last night I slept with a woman/ who was not my wife.
Kissed her like she was the last/ woman on earth I'd have
the pleasure of dying/ inside of. I used my tongue/ to write
a eulogy/ on her abdomen, saliva trickling down her thighs/
Face wet/ with her embalming fluid. Licking lips/ to
taste the afterlife. I lifted her mahogany legs/ like a
casket/ and wrote an obituary/ on her walls/ If I die here
tonight, then know it was on purpose/ Know everything
I did had intention. Each stroke/ was deliberate. Fierce/
Aggressive/ I pounded/ until I went numb. I pounded/ so I
could feel someone else coming/ alive.

Bankruptcy

My heart is a wallet
filled with everything
except the currency
which makes it worth carrying.
You will find statements shaped like love letters
marked with insufficient funds.
A bank slip attached to an empty vault
that refuses to unlock itself.

My heart is a ledger.
A red hyphenated balance
does not fade to black on its own.
It needs something to make it believe
that transition is possible.
This heart has suffered so many withdrawals
the residuals have sucked the interest out of my smile.

My heart is a weapon
I wield like a shard of glass afraid
of hurting myself by holding it incorrectly.
This house of vein and blood
can't renovate itself.
Most days I am a sledgehammer
with no handle to steer me.
A wrecking ball with no wall to plow through.
A husband with no wife.

Sonnelegy: In Peace

Grief has an uncanny ability
to cause paranoia. Makes you wonder
if God took your wife, then maybe he has
a price tag on your head too. Or perhaps
death is a bounty hunter with daddy
issues starving for God's sole attention.
I find scattered traces of my wife
in random places. A few months ago,
I heard her voice in a child's golden laugh.
Last week, I saw her eyes in the face of
one of my students. Today, I tasted
her tears when I answered my phone and heard
another black man had just lost his wife.
Tonight, I'll feel her as I dream, in pieces.

Instructions for the Day After a Long Night of Grieving

1. Awaken from the covers you caged yourself in last night
2. Reach to the left side of the bed
3. Wipe prayers off her leopard pillowcase when you realize she's not there
4. Punch the pillowcase once you realize she's still not
5. Sniff the pillowcase to remind yourself of how heaven once smelled
6. Scream
7. Scream louder until you're satisfied it reached God
8. Wrap the pillow around your face until breathing becomes optional
9. Choose breath
10. Breathe
11. Climb out of the bed
12. Glance at her bottle of oxycodone on the nightstand
13. Ask yourself if it's worth it
14. Swallow the oxy
15. Vomit the oxy
16. Place your hand over your heart
17. Look at the picture of her in wedding gown sitting on the nightstand
18. Tell her you love and miss her
19. Open her Spotify playlist
20. Sing off-key to Kirk Franklin while in the shower
21. Dance to the ratchet songs on that same playlist
22. Laugh at her duality
23. Leave shower
24. Put on the blue shirt and red and blue bowtie she loved the most
25. Spill into the creased khaki pants
26. Walk the dog
27. Leave home
28. Order a chicken minis combo from Chick-fil-A

29. Taste the nostalgia in each bite.
30. Arrive at work and say this is a good day
31. Remember that two months ago you couldn't get out of bed
32. Thank God for growth

Cry Yourself a Freedom Song

On the days when waking up
feels more burden than blessing,
heartache than healing,
When depression tap dances on the riot
in your throat, fear plays a sonata
in the key of disbelief,

remember,
there is gospel in your grief.
Every tear is a prayer.
So cry yourself a freedom song.
Sing a spiritual to the cadence
of your weeps.

Belt a hymn in the key of survival
and be thankful your melody
won't fall on deaf ears.

Praise

Today I will praise.

I will praise the sun

For showering its light

On this darkened vessel.

I will praise its shine.

Praise the way it wraps

My skin in ultraviolet ultimatums

Demanding to be seen.

I will lift my hands in adoration

Of how something so bright

Could be so heavy.

I will praise the ground

That did not make feast of these bones.

Praise the casket

That did not become a shelter for flesh.

Praise the bullets

That called in sick to work.

Praise the trigger

That went on vacation.

Praise the chalk

That did not outline a body today.

Praise the body

For still being a body

And not a headstone.

Praise the body,

For being a body and not a police report

Praise the body

For being a body and not a memory

No one wants to forget.

Praise the memories.

Praise the laughs and smiles

You thought had been evicted from your jawline

Praise the eyes

For seeing and still believing.

For being blinded from faith

But never losing their vision

Praise the visions.

Praise the prophets

Who don't profit off of those visions.

Praise the heart

For housing this living room of emotions

Praise the trophy that is my name

Praise the gift that is my name.

Praise the name that is my name

Which no one can plagiarize or gentrify

Praise the praise.

How the throat sounds like a choir.

The harmony in my tongue lifts

Into a song of adoration.

Praise myself

For being able to praise.

For waking up,

When I had every reason not to.

Vows II

Today is ▮ amazing ▮

▮ because ▮ you ▮

▮ are ▮

alive

I worship the queen in you

sing hallelujah

into the scripture that is your skin and read
you

bible chapter and verse

Definition

Widow(er)
Losing one's spouse through death. From Old English *widewe,* derived from Indo-European root meaning 'be empty.' i.e., an unleaded heart barren of its fuel is now *empty.* i.e., the indentation in satin sheet sits *empty* without the body that made it worth lying in. i.e., the glass is not half *empty or* half full, it no longer exists. i.e., cleanliness is next to godliness, but *emptiness* is next to nothing but itself. i.e., a full house without a body inside is still *empty.* i.e., the (wo)man has a mind full of memories and a calendar full of *empty* promises.

Root words:
'Wid' (meaning with) & *'Owe'* (meaning being indebted to). i.e., God *owes* me. i.e., God should repay me for the life he took *wid* him and away from me. i.e., my soulmate resides *wid* me forever and I *owe* them everything.

Examples:
1. The widow(er) lost everything including themself.
2. Their spouse is gone but the widow(er) is still alive, sometimes.
3. The widow(er) is no longer married but also not single.
4. The married person says "thank God I'm not a widow(er). The divorced person says "I'm a widow(er) too. The single person says, "at least the widow(er) experienced love at all." The widow(er) says "at least" is never enough.

Synonyms: *survivor, perseverance*
Antonyms: *husband, wife, married, together, forever*

What Not to Say to a Widower

God doesn't make mistakes
I know exactly how you feel
You're still young
You have time to find someone else
At least you didn't have kids together
Be happy you didn't live through a divorce
It's your fault
You're not grieving enough
Stop posting her on Facebook
You still wear your wedding ring?
The best way to get over her
is to get under someone else
Aren't you dating too soon?
It's time to move on
Be strong
She was sick anyway
What about her clothes?
Can I have her perfumes and lotions?
At least you were with her for 9 years
Enjoy your freedom
I can't date a man in love with a dead girl
I can never compare to her
Your poems will be so much better now
You don't look depressed
Everything happens for a reason
You're not married anymore
Ok we get it, she's dead

Anger

is a wall dripping with
blood from a stubborn hand.
Knuckles skinned from breaking
something that didn't hold a pulse.

TypeCast
for Elizabeth Olsen

The actress who plays Wanda Maximoff
in the show *WandaVision* also starred as Leigh
in the Facebook series *Sorry For Your Loss*.
In both shows she loses her husband tragically.

In one, her husband's skin is the same color as mine.
Copper tinted hands grab her pale flesh
in the most Loving way possible.
His melanin holds the sun like an affair.
He kisses her with an obituary on his breath
Looks at her like an apology he's too afraid to give.

In the other, her husband is a machine
designed to destroy the dirt beneath them,
but decides to avenge the darkness
rather than reside in its shifty hand.
He is both hero and villain
depending on who controls the wires.

Leigh spirals into mini bottles and random hookups,
a lost traveler in search of a legend to guide her home
Wanda kidnaps a town to create an alternate universe
where her husband is as alive as her memories.
Elizabeth is the body chosen to inhabit both souls.
A conjuring of wild magic that brings dead things back whole.

I wonder how it feels to play grief so well,
they only cast you as a dead man's relic.
To be a binge worthy-sensation
when sorrow is the storyline.

Alive

On the day she passed away, I fell
to my knees when I saw her body
sprawled across the hardwood.
Arms extended like the savior we prayed to
the night before.

As the casket folded over her flesh a week later,
a piece of me jumped inside of it with her.
A corpse searching for a morgue to house the dead
parts of me that refuse to live.

The word widower is a cancer
metastasizing each time the sun awakens.
It is a title no man wants to answer to.
A label no thirty-three-year-old man should have.

I'm confined to only seeing my wife
in the two videos on my cell phone,
five hundred pictures in a photo album,
ten thousand two hundred and twenty-five text messages,

two wedding DVDs,
and one voicemail I listen to religiously
to remind me of the heaven in her voice.
Losing her light makes darkness a more comfortable residence.

There's an apartment complex in my chest,
a god complex in my neck,
and the devil stands outside
offering complimentary valet service.

There are many days
I want to slide in the passenger side and buckle
my seatbelt for the rapture,
But I've always had this thing
about giving up all my things to other things.

So I hold onto the little bit of holy I have left,
and pray that Jesus is an Uber driver
who can chauffeur me to the gates of Heaven
and show me the place where my wife's smile still lives.

Her body finally free of all its scars.
Her heart as pure as it was
on the night we both said *I Do.*

My Wife is Dead

My wife is dead.
She is not living anymore.
She is with god.

My wife is living with god.
She is dead.
She is not living.
She is not anymore.

She is not my wife anymore.
She is dead god.
She is more dead than wife.
She is dead, god.

My wife is with god.
My wife is god.
More God than dead.
More God than god

She is dead. God.

The Last Gift

I gave Jasmine was a puppy for her birthday.
Once a month for eight years straight she'd ask,
and my reply was always *yeah one day babe,*

in attempt to satisfy her warm desire
and escape two more hours of interrogation.
Her eyes would cut kitchen knife sharp

when these words stumbled
off my nervous tongue.
I knew her patience came with an expiration date.

So when I told her the time had finally come,
her face danced into a jubilant smile.
Cheeks extended, exposing the whiteness of her teeth.

There was nothing but happiness there.
No hospital beds or coroners on our doorstep.

Two weeks later we journeyed down
a long road to pick up the dog.
When she sauntered on four legs towards us,

my wife's face started to dance again.
Swooned like a girl being asked to prom
for the first time. She picked up and cradled her

like the child she thought we'd never have,
and they two-stepped and spun in a circle
swaying to a song no one else could hear.

My wife gazed into the infant's eyes
and said "you're coming home,
you're finally coming home," and the pup

looked up as if she already knew this.
Dug paws into her mother's brown skin
ready to claim her place.

For the next thirty days
they were conjoined at the hip,
as if they knew their time had an expiration date.

I watched them play and jump, and saw the woman
who stole my heart have hers hijacked
by this unsuspected blessing.

There was only happiness here.
No EMTs or coroners on our doorstep.

On the day before my wife took
her last sabbatical in a hospital bed,
we placed our child in foreign hands.
A temporary fostering, lending our gift
to fingers who could hold her properly.
In the hospital a different set of hands

were unraveling my wife's wounds
trying to re-stitch her quilt of flesh.
Mending the brokenness through clenched jaw
and tear-soaked sheets.
Hours fade into darkness and the next day I
retrieve our bundle of four-legged joy
alone.

Vows III

Today

                                                          you are alive

This

                                   will not be

50

forever

Black Girl Fly

My girl is fly
    And not fly as in helicopter
    or airplane,
    or kite cascading across a sunset
    I mean
fly
    as in dope, fresh, trendy, sexy
So fly
    the wind asks her for permission to speak
So fly
    NASA consults her before
    sending shuttles beyond this galaxy
Fly
    like black birds somersaulting
    on a blue playground of sky
Fly
    like stiletto heels tall enough
    to reach heaven's backyard
Fly
    like walking into a room
    and stealing the spark in everyone's faces,
    turning any venue into a runway
Fly
    like she came to slay everything
    and all you can do is watch
    yourself become prey
So fly
    every follicle of hair is laid like a prayer
    bowing to the temple of her edges

So fly
> she convinces me to buy her
> sundresses every summer,
> like spending my money is her favorite pastime
> She'll flash a smile and say "Ang" in a tone that weakens
> the grip on my wallet and serenades the crease
> of my lips into a smile can't I resist

So fly
> I never complain
> I gladly carry anything
> her flesh leaves an imprint on

My girl is so fly
> she makes me believe gravity
> doesn't have jurisdiction
> over this blanket of flesh
> and flight is our native tongue

So fly
> she makes a hospital gown
> look like Fashion Week

So fly
> the nurses at CMC Pineville
> know her by name,
> greet her with a smile that says
> *I hate you're back here*
> *but I'm also happy to see you pop*

So fly
> she's had more surgeries
> than birthday parties

So fly
>
> the doctors gave her six months to live
> and she refused to stick to their timeline

So fly

> She talks to God on a first name basis,
> and writes a gospel with her tongue

Night Sky: 34.1954° N, 82.1618° W
Ekphrastic of a telescopic image of the sky on our wedding
night

Two lone stars dance
into a solar system of uncertainty.

Underneath a dark blanket of sky, the stars hold hands
and speak in supernova stanzas.

The brightest one glows a galaxy in her smile,
while the other bathes in the residual light she leaves.

Their touch a convergence of breath and sweat,
building a constellation even the moon is jealous of.

They are the brightest tandem the sky has ever given birth to.
Celestial coordinates freely spilling into each other,

two-stepping in the name of a love
they know they are becoming.

EpithaLITmium

There is no greater feeling than listening to 808s
spill their harsh calligraphy on a stereo,
while coasting down a South Carolina highway
There's something about passing old cotton fields
while listening to Three Six Mafia
that makes you feel a strange sense of comfort

When you turn your head to the passenger seat
and see your bride rapping the words
"slob on my knob, like corn on the cob,"

you laugh uncontrollably
You laugh because you realize the saying is true:
All pretty girls really do love trap music
You laugh even harder
because you remember the first time
you told a girl you loved her,
and she turned you down

You remember how it felt to have your heart muted
when you were full of so much music.
Your symphony of excitement put on pause
when she rejected you for a boy
who could never appreciate the cadence in her collarbone.
It took a while to find your rhythm,

but you found it
in a woman with turntables in her dimples.
Scratching the soundtrack to your heart
every time she cracked a smile
The melody made you believe in music again.
One day you turned down the volume
and asked to remix her last name

She said yes
And now you're both riding down a back road
screaming *check in with me, and do your job*
in unison. As though synchronicity is second nature
Like this is the duet you were waiting for all along.

Ode to my Wedding Ring

You taught me that these fingers are not
only valued when they contort into fist,
or bloodied from folding cheek into jawbone.
These hands are made to carry you like a sword.
A weapon we disguise as jewelry.
You grip me fiercely. Relentlessly.
You are worth more than the paychecks
she slaved for to purchase you.

My hands were trembling
until your silver lips kissed my molasses skin.
This must be what Deja vu looks like.
A reunion with something I never met,
but somehow have known the whole time.
I have been infatuated since
the clerk at Zale's pulled you out
of a glass case and slid you onto my naked hand.

You have slept on icy floors in hospital rooms,
somersaulted across the billowing sands
of Myrtle Beach, and pressed against flesh
to hold the body that made you possible.
How lovely it has been to gaze at your glow
and know I have been monogamous,
never prostituting my love for comfort.

True love is the mark you leave on my index finger,
the eight stones in your frame
to represent the eight years of her love.
It is the fear I feel when I think I've lost you.
The relief I taste when I realize I didn't.

You are the reason why
I decided to run after love. To chase.
To be exhausted and weightless at the same time.
Engaged without abandonment.
You are a symbol most would die to get
but not give their lives to keep.

Bargaining

is asking the cemetery
to unswallow the body.
begging the bullet to undo
the skull it made into mausoleum.

Vows IV

God

     I

        refuse

            to

                let

                    go

Blue

I never learned how to swim.
I almost drowned at a pool party
in the 6th grade.
I was the only dark body there.

When I saw the ivory colored kids
somersault off diving board
into the cold sanctuary below,
I wanted to feel what they felt.

To be free enough and safe enough
to jump into something that could kill me.
So I jumped and quickly sank,
until my arms were flailing ferociously

trying to grab onto something I couldn't see
like God or love. For a moment I felt weightless.
A black boy bird flying with no restraint
until the water reminded me I was human.

I have a hard time remembering
when I fell in love
with water. Truly don't recall the moment
waves enchanted my innocent eyes

and unearthed new worlds in these pupils.
Perhaps, it was in elementary school
when I was scribbling outside the lines.
When I had not yet become

acquainted with the burden of barriers.
Was not familiar that dark lines
were a thing you were not supposed to cross.
At that age we glided crayon across paper

with no intention of halt. Danced
over barricades until we made them beautiful.
We would dig our hands
in warm sand and soft beach,

submerging feet beneath the blue
until we could no longer see where we stood.
I loved the feeling of enveloping myself
in something larger than myself.

In college
a brown skinned girl with a sharp tongue
and soft smile taught me
how to float in the water.

To glide and extend limbs in a straight line
until my body turned still.
She was also instructing me in a crash course on love.
The art of stretching out and leaping

until joints tire of exhaustion.
To jump off of faith
into a pool of uncertainty.
I vowed to always study the aquatics of her.

So when I visit the cemetery
that now houses her bones,
I stare at the lake that surrounds her.
Use these sea legs

to swim to her gravesite
and extend my arms
like a black bird
trying to spread its wings.

Outer Space

When I was born
God gave me an assignment.
He said, there is an angel whose halo is so bright,
One day she will literally knock the wind out of you.
Two decades later I lost my breath
the first time you said my name,
And these lungs haven't been the same ever since.

I still remember the night we met.
When you walked into a dark room with all that light
I swear I saw our future develop
Like a film strip right in front of me
You strolled in with supernovas in your stilettos,
Large galaxies in your eyes
And I've been stargazing ever since.

One day you allowed me to gift you my last name.
Told me yes when you had every reason not to.
And one day you left.

On the day God evicted your body
from this planet I died too,
And that was the second time you took my breath away.

Cento: Acceptance?

is the God who rides shotgun
skipping to a rhythm no one knows.
The kid at school who we acknowledge
is ignoring the bully everyone is afraid of.
A melanated road map of sacrifice.
A freedom song in the key of survival.

Alternate future in which my wife is alive
For Cadence and AJ

My wife is lying in bed
while I am downstairs preparing breakfast:
Cheese grits, eggs, bacon, and mimosas.
An alchemist spinning memories with a frying pan
and bottle of champagne.

I place the food on the finest
china we have in the house.
The steam rises
off the feast into a cloud of gentle smoke,
briskly jogging up the stairs
faster than my excitement.

I walk into the room
just as her eyes
shake hands with the sunlight.
Happy Anniversary babe I yell,
with a mouth full of promise.

She quickly says it back,
wearing the same smile she did ten years prior.
I place the plate in her lap and watch
her bless the meal.
Each bite a thank you note
written on her taste buds.

Soon, we hear footsteps quickly sprint
from across the hall, and a boy

whose eyes look hungry for attention
jumps on the bed. *Where's my plate daddy?*
he asks with open-faced smile,
and I shrug shoulders
as though no answer exists.
My wife chuckles so hard
she clutches her stomach
to contain this joy.
She then snatches my hand
placing it on swollen belly
to feel what lies beneath.

You feel that? she asks
as I expose gums and bright teeth.
I guess she wanted to join in too
my son says, as he now lays palm
on the holy grail of flesh before him.
He says that it feels like she is dancing
inside a lonely ballroom ready to escape.

I pull my wife out of bed and play
Chocolate High, the song
we had our first dance to.
We two-step to the rhythm
of the trapped dancer's heartbeat.
I slowly spin her around and she says
boy I can't turn like I used to
and our son clenches her waist
to help her complete the revolution.

I turn my hand loose and instruct him
on how to dance with the woman.
To hold hand steady
and move until her hips sway
an ocean of calm.

Later we watch wedding DVDs,
look through photos and recite vows
from memory. Two lovers no longer
young yet anxious for more time.

Notes

Cry Yourself A Freedom Song: An earlier version of this poem appears in the *Thoughts on the Power of Goodness* (Chapel Hill Press, 2020).

Blue, Bargaining & Bankruptcy: Each of these poems appear in Jasper Writes

Praise: Earlier versions of this poem appeared in *Charleston Currents*, Gratefulness.com, and The Academy of American Poets 'Poem-a-Day' series, June 15, 2020.

Black Girl Fly: An earlier version of this poem won the *Fall Lines-A Literary Convergence* Saluda River Poetry contest and was published in the literary magazine's October 2021 issue.

Vows I, II, III & IV: These are erasure poems using the language of my vows from my wedding on Sept. 17, 2016.

Acknowledgements

This collection was truly a labor of love not only from myself, but from many others who lent care and attention to me and the poems themselves over the course of the past year and a half. First, I'd like to thank the quarantine (seriously) for allowing me the opportunity to slow down and actually put pen to paper on this collection. I thought my debut collection would be completely different, but once I allowed the words and process to happen naturally the work I was intended to create was born.

Thanks to my family, especially Mama, Trois, & Chelle for always being supportive and seeking to understand and respect my process even when it may not have made any sense to you. Thank you for attending every slam, open mic, reading and feature. That support has helped me become the man and artist I am today.

I am thankful to the countless teachers, writers and poets who have cultivated my skills and talents into what it is today. I am specifically thankful to the Concrete Generation, Respect Da Mic, Skinny Bully and Slam Charlotte. Those teams challenged me as a writer and a person. Thankful to the poetry slam community for accepting me, embracing me, and providing a platform to express myself.

Special thanks of course to Cindi Boiter and the good folks at Muddy Ford Press for believing in me as a writer and having faith in the work even when I didn't have faith in myself. It is no coincidence that my work is in your capable hands. It is so fitting that a press in my hometown would be the conduit for me giving birth to my first literary work.

Thanks to the amazingly talented Keela Lewis for the incredible artwork you created for the cover. It is truly behind my wildest dreams. You are simply gifted. To Jericho Brown-I appreciate your friendship and tough love. It is needed and appreciated more than you know. Thank you for that and for your kind words. To Marjory Wentworth-you are a giant of a woman whom I truly respect. Thank you for introducing me to Muddy Ford and agreeing to write a blurb for this collection.

I am truly forever indebted to my friend, colleague, and fellow Poet Laureate Ed Madden for editing the collection. Your suggestions and insight were intentional and careful but blatantly honest. You challenged me to make the necessary revisions and edits that would elevate the collection to the space where it currently stands.

I seriously need to thank a handful of amazing writers who saw early versions of this manuscript and provided some valuable feedback which helped the collection transform from what it was to what it currently is. Those persons are Ephraim Sommers, Wendy Jones, and Junious "Jay" Ward. Each of you gave some meaningful feedback which both affirmed and pushed me. I'd especially like to thank Jay for being my right and left hand in this process. Jay you're an incredible writer and I'm honored to call you, my brother.

Thank you to The Watering Hole for allowing me to serve on the Board of Directors. Being a part of this amazing organization has truly meant a lot to me. I am thankful for the space you create for me and so many others In particular I'd like to thank my 2020 Retreat manuscript coaching cohort: Siaara Freeman, Noor Ibn Najam, Daniella Toosie-Watson, Michael Frazier, Junious "Jay" Ward, and our facilitator the incomparable Tyehimba Jess for giving some dynamic feedback on the manuscript. It pushed me to not settle and go the extra mile. I can't wait until your manuscripts become books in the world.

Thanks to the City of Rock Hill for allowing me to serve as your Poet Laureate. This tenure has truly been an amazing experience and I look forward to doing my part to help the city ascend to the space where it belongs.

Special thanks to my love Lula for allowing me space and time to create this work. Ironically, it took meeting you to unearth these poems. To me that's a co-sign! I appreciate you giving me space to grieve and being right there with me even when it may have been tough for you. Your immense support and commitment truly mean the world to me. I love you.

Thank you to the Jackson-Byrd family for always being supportive and loving me through this journey of widowhood. Losing a daughter/auntie/sister/niece/ isn't easy but you've embraced me like one of your own since day one. There are no words that can describe what that means to me.

74

Last, but certainly not least I'd like to thank my late wife Jasmine for allowing me to be her husband and blessing me with the time we shared on this rock we call earth. This collection is a monument to you and the impact you've had on my life. I am eternally thankful. The years go by faster, but the pain of your loss doesn't get any duller. Keep watch over all of us.

CPSIA information can be obtained
at www.ICGtesting.com
Printed in the USA
JSHW041439020622
26479JS00003B/11

9 781942 081302